This book belongs to:

Turtle and Guy

A Jeremy and Jazzy Adventure

Inspired by the song "Turtle and Guy"
by Jeremy Fisher

Based on the teleplay by Jeremy Fisher,
Robert de Lint, and Virginia Thompson

CORAL GABLES

Cover Design: Chris Morris
Cover Photo/illustration: Vérité Films in association with Smiley Guy Studios
Layout & Design: Chris Morris

For permission requests, please contact the publisher at:
Mango Publishing Group
2850 S Douglas Road, 4th Floor
Coral Gables, FL 33134 USA
info@mango.bz

For special orders, quantity sales, course adoptions and corporate sales, please email the publisher at sales@mango.bz. For trade and wholesale sales, please contact Ingram Publisher Services at customer. service@ingramcontent.com or +1.800.509.4887.

Turtle and Guy: A Jeremy and Jazzy Adventure

Library of Congress Cataloging-in-Publication number: 2022946597
ISBN: (print) 978-1-68481-218-9, (ebook) 978-1-68481-219-6
BISAC category code: JNF011000, JUVENILE NONFICTION / Careers

Printed in China

To my daughters Elsie and Hazel

Your laughter is music to me.

Hello, Fellow Readers!

Thank you for picking up this book and joining us on our musical adventures. In our world, there's a story in every song. Come explore how feelings become songs, songs become stories, and music and friendship create joy.

You can also watch the animated "Turtle and Guy" adventure, listen to our music, or discover how you can learn with us by scanning the QR code below.

We can't wait for you to join us!

Your friends,
Jeremy and Jazzy

Turtle

Guy

There's a guy named Turtle
and a turtle named Guy,
share a little house
on the lower east side.

Nap all day, sleep all night.
A guy named Turtle
and a turtle named Guy.

In the town where they write the *Toronto Star* paper,
a land of apartments and super skyscrapers,
was Turtle and Guy's house.

It didn't fit in.
And in that way this house
was a bit like our friends!

Their friendship was strong.
The best! Things were awesome!
But they kept running into
the same old problem.

There'd be a ring-a-ding-ding
from the phone on the wall
or a letter at the door,
written in scrawl.

Mr. Turtle Guy was
the name it was for.
Was it Turtle or Guy?
They couldn't be sure.

Guy said, "Turtle, I totally agree.
Is the letter for you? Or is it for me?"

They managed together
and got by okay
until the announcement
of a big prize one day.

The winner was random,
plucked out of the sky.
The name on the ticket...

Mr. Turtle Guy?

Things got mixed up!
They were not amused!
Whenever this happened
they felt...

CONFUSED!

There's a guy named Turtle
and a turtle named Guy,
share a little house
on the lower east side.

Nap all day,
sleep all night.
A guy named Turtle
and a turtle named Guy.

Oh, why oh why?

They examined the ticket for some kind of clue.

Turtle said, "Guy, I hope it's for you!"

With a magnifying glass he pulled out of his shell,

Guy said,

"I hope it's for you as well!"

The big boss of the prize
was as mad as a hatter!
He grabbed it and said,
"What the WHAT
is the matter?"

"Clearly the big prize
must go to the winner.
Mr. Turtle Guy's the name
that came out of the printer."

The printer said,

"But, but, but... I only do what I'm told!

I printed the name and outlined it in gold!

It's the computer who sent me the names.

It's the computer who should take the

BLAME."

The computer said,
"The names are all part of a list in a system
that came from the big boss's trusty assistant.
I couldn't have changed them, even if I tried.
I'm programmed to do it the same every time."

The boss blew a gasket
and threw his hands in the air.

"There are rules to this prize!
We've got to be fair!
Where is this list?
What is this system?
Who gave the go-ahead
to my assistant?"

Things were mixed up!

He was not amused!

Whenever this happened he felt...

There's a guy named Turtle
and a turtle named Guy,
share a little house
on the lower east side.

Nap all day,
sleep all night.
A guy named Turtle
and a turtle named Guy.

Oh, why oh why?

The big boss stood up on a soapbox he found
to get their attention and calm the crowd down.
"I hear you, my friends. I guess I didn't understand.
It seems Mr. Turtle Guy

isn't ONE man."

"The mistake is mine. I've made some before.
I admit I was wrong, so let's settle the score."

"But the thing I can't change is...
there's only one prize.
I don't know for sure if it's

Turtle's or Guy's!"

Just then the big boss
looked down below.
Guy was tap-tapping
him on his big toe.

"Please sir, just tell us.
What is the big prize?"

Everyone turned
and it lit up their eyes!

A shiny red bike
with a bell and a basket!
And presenting the ride
was rock star Joel Plaskett!

"Well, don't you think that it would be fair if Turtle and Guy took the bike and just shared?"

Hip hip and hooray!

Problem solved indeed!
The boss and the town
and our heroes agreed!

They rode into the sunset
with a ding of the bell.
And that's the whole story.
There's no more to tell!

Jeremy and Jazzy Adventures wishes to thank everyone involved in the creation of the original animation on which this book is based.

Animation Services Provided By

smiley guy
STUDIOS

Executive Producer
JONAS DIAMOND

Production Managers
CHRIS HERON
SARA LINARES ARBELÁEZ
MICHAEL REBELLATO

Animatic Editor
TOM BERGER

Storyboard Artists
LUKE COLEMAN
CAT ZYGOCKI

Character Concept Lead
IZZY ABREU

Background Concept Lead
PAUL HAMMOND

Character Designers
GREG HUCULAK
HALEY ROSE

Additional Character and Prop Designers
ANDREW BLONDIN
JUAN G. CORREA
ROSSI GIFFORD
PETER HABJAN
MIKE LININGTON
APARAJITA RAVICHANDRAN

Rigging Supervisors
POLINA KOTLIAR
JOSEPH LAGUE

Rigging Team
ANDREW FLEMING
AJA LOMOVIC
DORIELLE RETEMYER
LEA MacDONALD
ADAM UJHELYI

Colour Concept Designers
ALEX BAYLISS
JOEL CHAHAL
AARON HONG
ARAMIKA KLIAVIN

Background Supervisor
PAUL HAMMOND

Layout Artists
BEN ROBOLY
ADAM WAITO

Background Painters
PAIGE DONER
UNA DI GALLO
SAM LAUZON

Additional Background Painters
ALEX BAYLISS
ANDY MALE
BEN ROBOLY
ALLAN TODA
ADAM WAITO

Set Up Supervisor
CHANTELLE SCHRIVER

Compositing Supervisor
MARC FORTIN

Compositors
HEIN SCHLEBUSCH
EVA YU

Online Compositor
JOEL GREGORIO

Traditional Animators
AISHA GHALI
MIKE LININGTON

Animation Supervisor
JASON HALL

Animators
SEAN BRANIGAN
MATTHEW BURROWS
AVRIL CHENGEHVY
JUAN G. CORREA
COLTON CULLEN
JENNIFER ELDRACHER
VANESSA FARDOE
ANDREW FLEMING
RAINIE GUO
JESSE ILG
AJA LOMOVIC
ADAM MASSICOTTE
DORIELLE RETEMYER
NOEL RUPPENTHAL
KURTIS SCOTT
JOHN TIELLI
THOMAS TWOLAN
DANI WOODS
KING XIONG
DI YAO
ZACK ZAND

FX Supervisor
POLINA KOTLIAR

FX Animators
AJA LOMOVIC
DORIELLE RETEMYER

Jeremy and Jazzy Adventures created by

JEREMY FISHER
ROBERT de LINT
VIRGINIA THOMPSON
"PARKSIDE" MIKE RENAUD

Special Thanks To

AGNES AUGUSTIN
BECKI BRISSON
ROD BUTLER
SWIN CHANG
CAMEILE HENRY
DANIELLE HEBERT
MATT HILLIARD-FORDE
ANISHA JAMAL-CADENA
NANCY LAING
JAMIE MACKAY
ROSA R. MAILU-NIROMAHEA
BEN MARIANO
MARIE MCCANN
STUART MCCARDIE

KYRA MILLAN
CATHY NOSATY
AIZA NTIBARIKURE
MATT OUIMET
JOEL PLASKETT
SLAIGHT MUSIC
PAUL QUIGLEY
OKO SHIO
PATRICIA VOLK
EMA WORSLEY
STAFF AND STUDENTS
AT SHERIDAN COLLEGE

DragonFruit, an imprint of Mango Publishing, publishes high-quality children's books to inspire a love of lifelong learning in readers. DragonFruit publishes a variety of titles for kids, including children's picture books, nonfiction series, toddler activity books, pre-K activity books, science and education titles, and ABC books. Beautiful and engaging, our books celebrate diversity, spark curiosity, and capture the imaginations of parents and children alike.

Mango Publishing, established in 2014, publishes an eclectic list of books by diverse authors. We were named the Fastest-Growing Independent Publisher by Publishers Weekly in 2019 and 2020. Our success is bolstered by our main goal, which is to publish high-quality books that will make a positive impact in people's lives.

Our readers are our most important resource; we value your input, suggestions, and ideas. We'd love to hear from you—after all, we are publishing books for you!

Please stay in touch with us and follow us at:

Instagram: @dragonfruitkids

Facebook: Mango Publishing

Twitter: @MangoPublishing

LinkedIn: Mango Publishing

Pinterest: Mango Publishing

Sign up for our newsletter at www.mangopublishinggroup.com and receive a free book! Join us on Mango's journey to change publishing, one book at a time.